Understanding Marx and *Capital*

Denis Collin - Yves Rouvière

Understanding Marx and *Capital*

COMPRENDRE/ESSAI GRAPHIQUE

1

A Life's Journey

To understand anything about Marx, the first thing to do is surely to forget Marxism, to leave aside, at least temporarily, everything that has been said about "Marxist economics", "Marxist philosophy", "historical materialism" and "dialectical materialism". "I'm not a Marxist", exclaimed the man his family and friend Engels called the "Moor", because of his dark complexion and jealous nature. Of course, there's the context: Marx was talking about those who called themselves "Marxists" in France, Lafargue and Longuet, his two sons-in-law, "the last Bakuninist and the last Proudhonian", "the plague take them!" But the joke went a long way. Marx has been swallowed up by Marxism. Rather like the statue of the god that Plato evokes in Book X of *The Republic*: having

remained at the bottom of the sea for so long, the statue of Glaucus looked more like a wild beast than a god.

Marx is not a god. He is not immortal—only atoms are immortal, he told his doctor in Algiers. We could forget this German émigré who lived pennilessly, writing about money and capital, and now rests in London's Highgate Cemetery. Forget him, or keep him in a museum of the bygone industrial age. Wasn't Mr. Marx a philosopher of the steam age? And if the bourgeoisie occasionally scare each other by announcing Marx's return, it's because it's not that serious. The salons are boring. But there's more. We've all, more or less, learned a few frustrating bits of doctrine: infrastructure determines superstructure, capitalism is a system of worker exploitation, and so on. But these typical phrases cannot sum up the thinking of this man who read every book and wrote thousands of pages in his illegible handwriting, authorizing only sparingly the publication of forewords, prefaces and other introductions to the "critique de l'économie politique" that occupied him for forty years.

After the death of his wife Jenny, née von Westphalen, Marx, whose health was steadily deteriorating, was sent to the sun by his doctor. He crossed France by train, then embarked for Algiers. On his return, he stopped off in

Cannes, Monte Carlo and then at his daughters' homes near Paris, Laura's and Jenny's, who was soon to die of cancer. In Algiers, he talked with banished Communards exiled to the colonies, Proudhonians, Fourierists, all those varieties of "utopian socialism" whose death certificate he thought he'd signed thirty-five years earlier in the *Manifesto of the Communist Party*. But nothing is ever finished. A Fourierist from Algiers praised a community that was also a community of love, just as Charles Fourier had imagined it a few decades earlier... Utopia has a hard life.

On the train back from Marseille to Paris, then from Paris to London, the "Moor" has time to take stock of a life he knows is now at an end. Is there a guiding thread, something that holds this life together? The river meanders, but all rivers flow to the sea. From the young man who frequented the "Young Hegelians" in Berlin and wrote his doctoral thesis on "The Difference of Nature in Democritus and Epicurus", to the sick old man, sick from having been sick so often, sick from having offered his family only a life of privation, sick now from the death of his wife, the story of one of the most important philosophers unfolds. Important in terms of the publicity his writings received and their supposed influence on the course of world history, but also important intrinsically: for example, Michel Henry, a Christian philosopher inspired by Husserl's phenomenology and a merciless critic of Marxism, maintains that **Marx is one of humanity's greatest philosophers.**

MARX'S LIFE ALMOST ALWAYS MERGES WITH THE HISTORY OF THOUGHT. And as with all great philosophers, there are ruptures, reworkings and heart-rending revisions. There's no point in trying to fit everything into a twenty-line presentation to make an index card to revise for the baccalaureate! We can, however, find a guiding thread, an inspiration that never leaves Marx, a key word that enables us to understand the whole: ***emancipation***. In 1842, in the *Rheinische Zeitung* ("Rhineland Gazette"), he began to define his own political and philosophical positions. He spoke out on freedom of the press, and above all published an important article on the law on timber theft. Starting with the passage of a law prohibiting the gathering of dead wood in the woods—an ancestral practice analogous to gleaning—Marx began a critique of private property and initiated the movement that would lead him to communism. He began to contrast the rights of the rich and the rights of the poor. And he sided with the rights of the poor: "But it is also in its activity that poverty already finds its right. In gathering, the elementary class of human society asserts itself as a factor of order vis-à-vis the products of the elementary power of nature." **It is the activity of the poor that now**

«La première liberté de la presse consiste à ne pas être un commerce.» (Karl Marx, 1842)

constitutes the ordering factor of society as a whole. Marx considers the poor, who did not exist in the historiography of the time, to be the major actors in history. There was no longer any question of looking for a political organization in line with the ideal: what was essential was the practical activity of individuals, those men who freely made their own history, as he would soon say. "Philosophy of praxis", as Labriola and Gramsci put it, praxis being activity directed towards the transformation of social relations, not the production of things.

2

Crossing Appearances

As a radical democrat, Marx criticized democrats for failing to get to the root of things, contenting themselves with proclaiming abstract rights, the rights of an egoistic individual, the ideal member of bourgeois civil society, or that *homo economicus* of which today's economists make the atom of social and economic life. The revolutions of the eighteenth century—the American and the French—proclaimed liberty and equality, but liberty was revealed as the freedom to exploit offered to the few who owned, and the deprivation of liberty for the immense cohort of proletarians thrown into the furnace of the burgeoning capitalist mode of production. As for equality, it's only the formal equality of the buyer and seller of labor power who enter into the bargain: the buyer "takes the lead and, as a capitalist, walks first; the owner of the labor power follows behind as his own worker; this one with a smirking look, looking important and busy; this one timid, hesitant, reticent, like someone who has taken his own skin to market, and can only expect one thing: to be tanned".

The sleight of hand that turns freedom and equality into alibis for domination and exploitation must be exposed. Marx spent his life on this task: to understand the mechanisms of capital's domination, its power, but also what real, practical movement can abolish this domination. And to do this, we need to move beyond the discourse of law and morality, and look at what happens in the engine room, where people produce and reproduce the material conditions of their existence.

All known human societies are based on the division of labor and cooperation: it is the division of labor that makes cooperation possible, and the increase in labor productivity, which in turn enables further developments in the division of labor. If eight men are enough to produce enough food, clothing and lodging for ten, the last two will be able to do something else: administer the common affairs of the group, deal with the powers of nature and the gods, or become chiefs. How are the tasks assigned to each member, and how are the goods produced by the community distributed? It all depends. In sufficiently small,

Liberté, Égalité, Propriété.

blood-bonded societies, everyone is expected to do what they can, and is basically given what they need. And the surplus is exchanged with other groups by barter, or that refined and often misunderstood system of give-and-take, analyzed by ethnologists such as Marcel Mauss—there's good reason to believe that giving has long been more important than trading in the formation of social bonds. With the development of material production, agriculture and the construction of the first cities, another system emerged: producers worked independently of each other and offered the products of their labor on a market where they could meet those who needed them. The specific products of individual human labours began to take on the general form of commodities, which found their general equivalent in money or currency.

Why is understanding the nature of the commodity so important? Because it is the "cell" of capitalist society, i.e., it concentrates all the determinations that find their development in the modern societies that emerge from the Renaissance onwards, to such an extent that wealth and the commodity are considered equivalent. The wealth of our societies appears as an immense accumulation of commodities! This is obviously not the case in reality. Air, water, landscapes, soil resources, cultural heritage

and social traditions are all goods that characterize the wealth of individuals and nations. But the empire of the commodity has spread to such an extent that everything that does not appear as a commodity is not considered wealth, or is fictitiously converted into a commodity for valuation purposes.

"THE WORLD IS NOT A COMMODITY", PROCLAIMED THE "ALTER-GLOBALISTS". Pure proclamation! The world, our world, is the world of the commodity. Initially confined to the margins of the production of material life—the peasant sold only his surpluses in order to procure a few durable goods—commodity production has gradually invaded all areas of life, infiltrating every pore of society.

The general "commodification" of life finds its apotheosis in the domination of money. **Money is the general equivalent of all commodities. Through it, all goods can be compared, reflected in each other: a cell phone top-up and a pack of cigarettes are made equivalent. All differences are abolished. Not only do things become equal when they are incommensurable, but so do human activities: the work that produces a given object of use is a particular, concrete task, requiring very specific skills and efforts.** Money, by making all the products of human labor equivalent, trans-

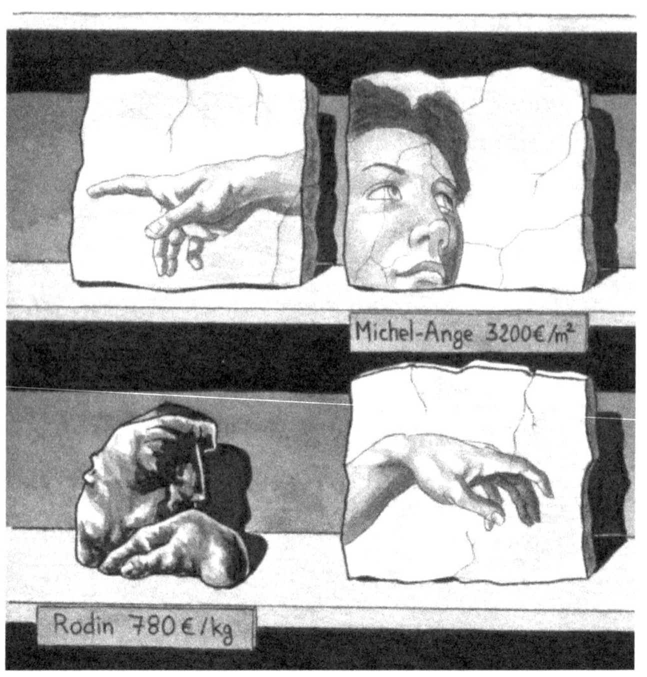

forms all human labor into general, abstract labor. Behind the apparent world of shimmering supermarket stalls, abstraction reigns. All the specific, concrete work that went into producing the cell phone or the pack of cigarettes is made equal, undifferentiated. The division of labor within the company, as in society as a whole, reduces productive activity to a simple expenditure of labor power, and as machines often render muscle power superfluous, work becomes a pure expenditure of time.

The traditional miser and the conquistador were driven by the "sacred hunger for gold" (*auri sacra fames*). Father Grandet, the Balzacian hero, had a yellow complexion from contemplating the coins he had accumulated. But this is a perverse use of money. Money circulates and makes things circulate. It circulates merchandise: the merchandise is sold and the money from this sale, immediately or much later, will be used to buy another merchandise. With money, I buy goods to resell them at a profit. As a means of exchange between commodities, money maintains equality: a bottle of alcohol or a copy of *Capital* are deemed equal on the market when they are exchanged for the same sum. But when it circulates, money does not remain equal to itself. It must "make little ones". The sum thrown into circulation must grow. Then, and only then, does money become capital.

MARX WELCOMED THE GREAT TRANSFORMATION OF MODERN TIMES. In the *Communist Manifesto*, his best-selling work, he extols the capitalist mode of production as the revolutionary mode of production par excellence. His communism is not the invention of a nostalgic dreamer of the golden age; it is the development of all the possibilities opened up by the reign of capital, once it has hopelessly broken all the bonds of subjection of traditional societies. And here we need to clear up a misunderstanding. A huge misunderstanding that prevents us from really understanding what Marx is saying. In caricatures, the capitalist is often depicted with his rich suit, top hat and fat cigar. He's paunchy, cynical and cruel. He's rolling in gold because he's starving the people.

A nineteen-hundreds libertarian newspaper like *L'Assiette au beurre* makes the capitalist and his servants (cops, priests, judges) prototypes of the sadistic pervert. The class struggle between workers and capitalists is thus a kind of struggle between the good poor and the evil rich, an eternal struggle of which cinema has given us so many versions. But *Capital is* not *The Seven Samurai.* **Marx is not concerned with the capitalist, but with capital, i.e. the gigantic social machinery that is constantly revolutionizing our societies, a revolution that does not spare the ruling class itself.**

How did this machinery come into being? We'll say a few words about that later. For now, it's enough to know the logic behind it. Simple commodity exchange—or "natural" exchange, as Aristotle would have said, to which Marx never fails to return—is the exchange of one commodity for another in order to satisfy needs: I sell what I don't need, but which must satisfy the need of another (who thus satisfies his need through my labor), in order to be able to buy what I need, i.e., to satisfy my need through the intermediary of another's labor. Simple commercial exchange is just the other face of the division of labor and cooperation between individuals to satisfy everyone's needs. But as soon as money ceases to be a mere means and begins to circulate as capital, everything is turned on its head. Far from money being used to satisfy needs, needs become the means to "make money". Life, which is normally the end of economic activity, becomes the means to an end, and the means, the pure means that is money, becomes the end in itself, it comes alive and becomes as if alive: it "makes little ones" as a father makes children—as Aristotle already said. Capitalism is the reversal of reality.

3

The Mysteries of Turning Money into Capital

This astonishing transformation conceals a secret. How can money "make babies"? As a general rule, goods are exchanged at their value. Fluctuations in supply and demand compensate each other statistically. Prices oscillate more or less around a pivot price, which corresponds to the value of the commodity. If I buy a commodity M for A and resell it, I should only get A (except in speculative situations, where I can make an exceptional "capital gain"). I can also lend my money against interest, but the borrower will only risk this operation if the loan is profitable for him, i.e. if he can earn money with the borrowed money and thus return capital and interest to the lender while keeping a profit for himself. Pawnbrokers and loan sharks who live off the misery of the world are marginal figures who stand in the interstices of traditional society, but they do not foreshadow the modern banker or the authentic capitalist.

We can turn the problem on its head: goods cannot increase in value as they circulate. To go a step further, we need to say a few words about this famous value. Goods have a use value: they correspond to a human need that they must satisfy. A Bible satisfies spiritual needs, and a bottle of cognac satisfies the need for spirits. These needs, in themselves, are immeasurable, and the goods that satisfy them have nothing in common in this respect. And yet, with the same amount of money, I could buy a bible (in a beautiful edition) or a bottle of cognac. **Money has miraculously equalized what was incomparable**. The exchange of goods through money has made these goods commensurable.

What determines the extent to which goods are reflected in each other? There are several answers. The oldest, that of Aristotle, is to say that if money makes incommensurable things commensurable, it is by virtue of a convention. This unconvincing answer reflects the state of a society in which the circulation of goods remains marginal. Marx takes up, before submitting it to criticism, the "labor-value" theory he found in English classical political economy: commodities are exchanged between themselves in proportion to

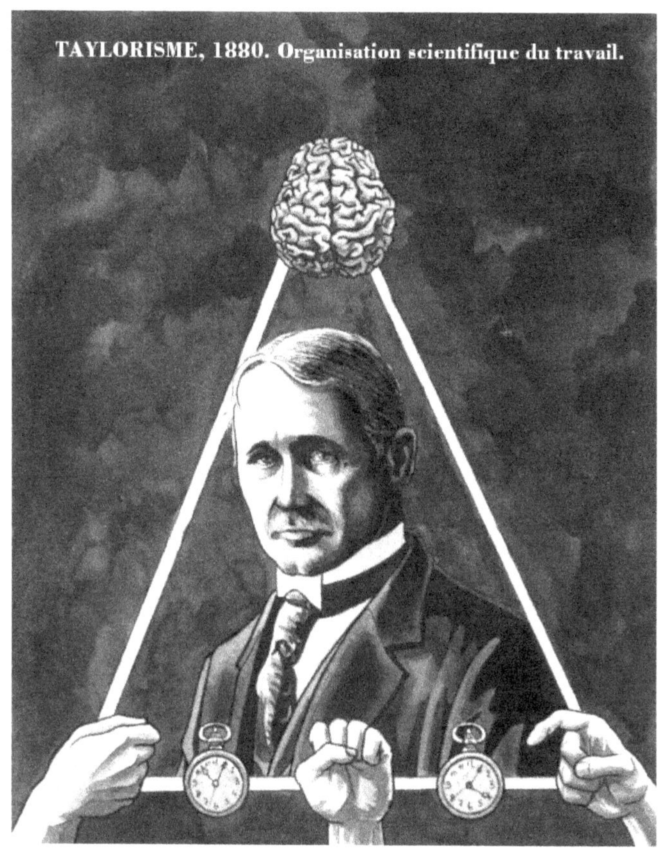

the average social labor time incorporated in them. This point is a little complex and needs to be developed. How, after all, can we compare human labor such as that of the vintner and the printer? The same difficulty we encountered when we wondered how to compare goods with completely different qualities now arises when we compare the actual work required to produce them! The answer, however, is quite simple: the development of the division of labor, on the one hand, and the habit of comparing the labor time required for production, on the other, have progressively reduced the diversity of human work to abstract labor time, the pure expenditure of labor power. The fragmentation of work with Taylorism makes this equivalence of human labor completely obvious, whatever the goods produced. Work of any kind is thus reduced to time.

ACADEMIC ECONOMISTS HAVE LITTLE LOVE FOR THE LABOR-VALUE THEORY. As market-oriented economists, they have little use for a theory focused on production. Practical capitalists, i.e. industrial entrepreneurs, take an entirely different view. Although they have learned the dogmas of marginal utility theory, when it comes to running their factories and producing goods, they rely on that accursed labor-value theory. They evaluate their relationship with the competition in terms of working hours. How long does it take to produce a Toyota in Japan, and how long does it take to produce an equivalent car in France? How can the time needed for production be reduced to keep up with the competition?

FORDISME, 1908. Standardisation et rationalisation du travail.

How can we increase labor productivity? Far from the clever mathematical models of economists—models that invariably fall apart with each new crisis—the practical capitalist knows that it takes labor time to produce the goods he puts on the market, and that his relationship with the competition will ultimately be a relationship between different labor times to produce the same goods.

There have been tons of books written on this question. But let's assume for the moment that Marx is right in saying that the value of a commodity corresponds to the abstract labor it incorporates. And here we must understand *abstract* in its most precise sense: abstract labor is labor insofar as we abstract from all its particularities, a labor stripped of everything that made it the manifestation of human vital activity, and which is reduced here to undifferentiated labor time, a pure quantity.

Let's return to the problem of the circulation of money, which allows it to function as capital. If I buy a commodity M for a sum A, I cannot resell this commodity A' (A plus a profit) unless, in passing through my hands, this commodity has undergone a mysterious transformation, so that when I resell it, it incorporates more social labor time than when I bought it. If I spend hours of labor modifying it before putting it into circulation, the problem remains. All I've done is add hours of labor to my merchandise, but those hours have cost me, and we're still left with the principle of equivalent-for-equivalent exchange. We'd have to find a commodity which, when consumed, would have the property of producing new value.

THIS MYSTERIOUS COMMODITY IS CALLED "LABOR POWER". Its seller is well known: the proletarian, who has nothing else to live on and goes to market to sell his hide—and can expect only one thing, to be tanned. The proletarian does not in fact sell his labor, but places his labor power at the capitalist's disposal for a fraction of the day fixed by contract, taking into account the laws and habits of the time and place. **What is the value of labor power? As with any commodity, its value is equivalent to the labor time incorporated into it, i.e. the time required for its "production".** Labor power requires a living individual to be fed, clothed and housed; it also requires training time—as minimal as possible once the division of labor has reached a sufficient point. So when the capitalist buys labor power, he must pay for it at its value, i.e. in proportion to the social labor time required to maintain it. Then, as with everything else he buys, he disposes of it as he sees fit. Let's suppose that the value of labor power is equivalent to four hours of social labor time (in four hours, the worker has produced goods whose value is equivalent to his wage). If this worker works for eight hours, he produces for his capitalist the equivalent of goods that incorporate eight hours of general human labor, whereas the capitalist has spent only four.

Labor power is therefore an extraordinary commodity: when the capitalist makes use of it, instead of being destroyed—as happens when ordinary commodities are consumed—it not only produces the equivalent of its replacement value, but also offers the capitalist free labor time. Let's summarize the process:

—The capitalist buys raw materials and machinery, the value of which he will factor into the calculation of his production costs; let's call "c" (as in "constant capital") the portion of capital spent for this purpose.

—He buys labor power, which we'll call "v" (for "variable capital").

—All these commodities (c + v) are thrown into the furnace of production, only to emerge metamorphosed (steel, plastic, etc., became automobiles, for example).

—The value of the commodities thus produced is equivalent to c + v, but to this must be added the free labor time enjoyed by the capitalist, which we'll refer to with

Marx's translators as "pl" (as in "surplus value" or "goodwill").

—In short, at the start of the production process, the sum of money functioning as capital is c + v, at the end it is c + v + pl. We can now explain how, by buying A a commodity M, we can then obtain A'. We had to buy a commodity whose consumption is productive.

Money has become a commodity because it has been converted into labor power. Those in the "engine room" of the capitalist mode of production are well aware that only human labor produces value... but seen from the outside, from the investor's point of view, it's money that "works": I make my money work," says anyone with money to "invest". The oldest forms of capital—such as loans with interest—now appear as derivative forms of truly productive capital, i.e. capital invested in the production of goods. Anyone who lends money to a capitalist entrepreneur will receive, in the form of interest, a share of the surplus value produced in production. The same applies to land rent: the landowner rents his land or buildings to someone who will include them in his production process— the capitalist farmer, for example. This is why the forms of interest-bearing capital and rent-bearing capital have long appeared to the industrial capitalist as parasitic forms: this

explains the sometimes violent conflicts between the various fractions of the ruling classes during the nineteenth century, as industrial capitalism sought to shake off the yoke of the old landed property (often attached to the nobility) and the bank.

4

Primitive Accumulation

ACCORDING TO MARX, FOR MONEY TO CIRCULATE AS CAPITAL AND THUS SET THE GENERAL DIRECTION OF SOCIAL LIFE, FOR MONEY TO BE REGULARLY TRANSFORMED INTO CAPITAL, A NUMBER OF SOCIO-HISTORICAL CONDITIONS MUST BE MET; these gigantic events are then quickly forgotten, and the capitalist mode of production appears as the natural mode of production.

FOR THIS PROCESS TO TAKE PLACE, capital accumulation had to reach a critical mass. The endogenous development of the capitalist mode of production in European cities was unable to reach this critical mass, even if we can trace the birth of proto-capitalism in the cities of Northern Italy at the end of the Middle Ages. Fernand Braudel shows that the accumulation of sufficient capital to ensure the development of the capitalist mode of production as the dominant mode of production cannot be achieved solely through the development of traditional commodity production. For this to happen, at least two fundamental conditions must be met. The first is the existence of masses of money ready to function as capital. By itself, small-scale merchant production cannot provide this, often because of the competition between different producers: the small shopkeeper, even if smarter or more industrious than his competitors, will rarely become a big capitalist, especially as all trades, organized into guilds, are governed by very strict rules. Long-distance trade, with its inherent monopolies, was the only means of accumulation. The arrival of modern times, with the conquest of the world by Europeans and the development of colonialism, provided the necessary ingredient for the development of capitalism. The "destruction of the Indies" recounted by Bartolomé de Las Casas in 1531 was the first chapter in **the story of capitalism's arrival in the world, sweating mud and blood from every pore.**

BUT CAPITAL WASN'T ENOUGH; it also required available labor power, i.e. "free" workers, i.e. free of all property, workers without tools, forced to sell their labor power on pain of starvation. Here again, the transformation of the ancient medieval working classes into the modern proletariat was not achieved by the immanent laws of the "free market", but by armed violence and massacres.

Elizabethan England was the scene of a veritable civil war waged by the *landlords* against the free British peasantry. Where peasant communities worked communal plots, the *landlords* erected fences (*enclosures*) to graze their wool-bearing sheep, intended as raw material for the burgeoning textile industry. As the old adage goes, what belongs to all belongs to none, the *landlords* were able to argue that they were not stealing from anyone by privatizing common land. Peasants, reduced to poverty, were soon driven from their homes *manu militari*: when they really didn't want to leave, villages were set on fire. In Scotland and Ireland especially, this led to terrible famines. Hundreds of thousands of wretched people were thrown onto the roads, reduced to begging or brigandage—Dickens' world was being built at the time. But depriving peasants of resources was not enough: they had to be forced to become "modern" workers. To this end, incipient "liberalism" resorted, as usual, to the coercive means of the state: the freedom of landlords presupposed the end of the freedom of peasants. The Poor Laws made it possible to hunt down beggars and lock them up in "*workhouses*", a kind of English-style labor camp.

1845, Ballinglass. Expropriation de dizaines de milliers de paysans pendant la grande famine.
1933, USA. Expropriation des paysans dans le Middle West pendant la Grande Dépression.

2004, Chine. Expropriation de 3 à 4 millions de paysans pour faire place à des projets industriels ou à la spéculation foncière.

2009, Afrique. 45 millions d'hectares changent de main suite aux investissements fonciers agroalimentaires et biotechnologiques...

When you reread this history, you can't help but compare the expropriation of the British peasantry to the forced collectivization imposed by Stalin in the early 1930s. Expulsion by armed violence, the destruction of peasant property (the former in favor of private capitalist property, the latter in favor of state property under the control of the ruling caste), famines and forced labor. That this comparison should be made at all speaks volumes about the exact nature of the Soviet Union: "primitive socialist accumulation" is the only carbon copy of primitive capitalist accumulation.

Elsewhere in Europe, the process was not as violent as in this paradise of so-called nascent "liberalism". But **everywhere, it was the destruction of the free peasantry and crafts that provided the material basis for the expansion of the capitalist mode of production.** It took time to transform these self-employed workers and beggars into disciplined proletarians. Police surveillance and the work book show that the sellers of labor power were hardly prepared to suffer their fate without protest. They kept the memory of their lost freedom alive, and this is what we find in the anarchist movements in Europe and the *"woobblies"* in the United States.

MARX ANALYZES THIS ORIGIN OF THE MODERN PROLETARIAT AND DRAWS THE CONSEQUENCES: the capitalist mode of production has expropriated independent workers. **The overthrow of capitalism must therefore be the expropriation of the expropriators and the restoration of individual property, but on the basis of socialized production.**

5

Exploited and Alienated

ACCORDING TO MARX, THE MECHANISM OF THE TRANSFORMATION OF MONEY INTO CAPITAL ENABLES US TO GRASP THE SPECIFIC MECHANISMS OF CAPITALIST EXPLOITATION AND SOCIAL DOMINATION. All historically known societies are class societies. Dominant classes impose their law on the dominated, who must work for the pleasure of the dominant. Until the 19th century, slavery was widely practiced. In the United States, it wasn't abolished until the eighteen-sixties, and then only at the cost of a civil war that claimed over six hundred thousand lives. The lords and dignitaries of the Church imposed their law on the serfs and peasants, and so on.

THE CAPITALIST MODE OF PRODUCTION COULD BE SEEN AS A CONTINUATION OF THIS ANCIENT OPPOSITION BETWEEN DOMINANT AND DOMINATED CLASSES. But this would be to miss the profound originality and revolutionary character of this mode of production. The ancient dominated classes were not made up of free men, but of subjugated men, who were often unable to control themselves and were bound by statutes that made them inferior to the dominant ones. The modern proletariat is made up of free men who are legally equal to their employers and enter into a free contract with them, concluded for the benefit of both parties. Freedom, equality, common utility: these are the main principles governing the buying and selling of labor power. In ancient forms of domination, the owners openly extorted labor from the dominated: to perform his chore, the serf would work for free for the lord several days a week. The relationships of domination are transparent. Not so in the capitalist mode of production. **The deal struck between buyer and seller of labor power is a seemingly fair one, in which no one is robbed. Free labor is concealed, and far from being the product of the worker's own activity, it appears as the legitimate fruit of capital.**

THE WORKER'S SITUATION IN THE CAPITALIST MODE OF PRODUCTION IS THEREFORE MARKED BY EXPLOITATION: part of the labor provided is monopolized by the capitalist. Marx calls the ratio of free labor to paid labor (the value of labor power) the rate of exploitation. Let's be clear: exploitation is not the result of

the actions of an evil capitalist; it follows from the logic of the system. The law of capital is the law of capital accumulation. The capitalist is not an unproductive consumer of the wealth produced by others—quite the contrary. The capitalist ethic is an ascetic ethic: enrichment is not for pleasure, but is its own end, and the capitalist's earthly mission is the indefinite pursuit of this enrichment. **The capitalist is the servant of capital," says Marx. So, if the individual capitalist exploits "his" workers, it is as a faithful servant of capital, i.e., as an agent of the "system".**

The development of capital requires that the rate of exploitation be maintained and even increased: not only because capitalists have no other choice in the face of competition, but also because the accumulation of capital reduces the share of living labor in the production process and tends to lower the rate of profit. Capitalism must simultaneously save living labor (increase its productivity) and preserve its profits, which depend solely on living labor. Marx devotes many pages to understanding these mechanisms, and this is exactly what he shows: it is the systemic logic of capital, and not the malice or greed of individual capitalists, that is to blame.

ONCE YOU ACCEPT THIS LOGIC, YOU HAVE TO DRAW THE CONSEQUENCES. All those who believe that capitalism is unsurpassable must admit it: for the system to continue to

plat
Notre économie a besoin
de   vous !!
Nouveau !! Le S
aloppes
porc!
€
TRAVAILLER PLUS

function, profits must be guaranteed, and as the source of profit is free labor, it is this "adjustment variable" that must be acted upon. Marx shows that an average rate of profit is established, and that it is in relation to this average rate that individual capitalists calculate their production costs. The least productive sectors will make profits below this average, while the most productive will pocket a surplus. **Surplus value is produced globally, and market competition between capitalists enables its distribution.** This is why every capitalist must, as a matter of life and death, take part in the race for surplus profit, which is also a race against the erosion of profits. And there are only so many ways to do this: increase working hours, raise labor productivity, lower the value of labor power.

For decades, workers' struggles focused on the legal limitation of the working day—a question that forms the central chapter of *Capital*. But "working more" is back on the agenda as an essential means of increasing "absolute surplus value", to use Marx's language. The race for productivity is the main driving force behind the technical development of the capitalist mode of production. Finally, the fall in the value of labor power can be achieved by reducing the value of the commodities necessary for the reproduction of labor power: for example, the relative value of foodstuffs has been falling steadily; in everyday language, the weight of food in the "housewife's basket" has been falling steadily. We could also mention the spectacular decline in consumer electronics. And this is why a reduction in the value of labor power can coexist with a more or less stable standard of living—thus, over the last few decades, the spectacular fall in the share of wages in per capita income has not led to a spectacular increase in poverty.

IN FACT, MARX ALWAYS OPPOSED THE THEORIES OF "PAUPERIZA-TION", WHICH HAD LONG BEEN PRESENTED AS A MARXIST PRINCIPLE. He always rejected Ricardo's thesis that wages should inevitably be reduced to the subsistence minimum. In his view, the value of labor power is socially fixed, and what is considered necessary for its reproduction varies according to social and historical conditions. Protection against illness and retirement have thus become part of the components of labor power, at least in the richest countries over the last half-century. But this is by no means a guarantee for the future—the gradual deconstruction of social protection systems is part and parcel of processes aimed at lowering the "cost of labor".

Once again, none of this has anything to do with the malignity of the owners. These are the immanent laws of the capitalist mode of production. When the owners of capital are institutions, the state or even employees (as in the case of pension funds), exploitation remains fundamentally unchanged.

BUT THERE'S ANOTHER DIMENSION TO THE SUBMISSION OF
LABOR TO CAPITAL: ALIENATION, an ambiguous term that
refers to the fact of no longer being oneself, of becoming a
stranger to oneself. The problem is not that the worker does
not receive the "full product of his labor". In no society,
however organized, can he. Part of it has to be set aside
for investment and research, and part has to be placed in
a pay-as-you-go fund for sickness, retirement and so on.
The problem is rather that the result of the worker's activity
stands up to him like a foreign power, that it appears as the
product of capital, and finally that the production process,
far from being the means the worker uses to achieve his
ends, becomes on the contrary an autonomous process, over
which the worker no longer has any control and of which he
is no more than a means. **When wage-earners take on
the name of "human resources", we reach the truth
of this process of alienation. Money in the form of
capital is presented as the lifeblood of society, while
workers are reduced to commodities, judged only by
their instrumental value.**

THE INCREASING FRAGMENTATION OF TASKS, THE INTERCHAN-
GEABILITY OF WORKERS AND THE DESTRUCTION OF TRADES ARE ALL
MANIFESTATIONS OF THIS GENERAL PROCESS, which machinism
expresses most acutely. The machine is the result of human

labor, but for the worker, it embodies capital—the capitalist is he who possesses the means of labor. As Marx puts it: "In machinism, the means of labor acquires a material existence that requires the replacement of human strength by natural forces, and of routine by science. [...] In the machine system, large-scale industry creates a completely objective or impersonal production organization, which the worker finds there, in the workshop, as the ready-made material condition of his work. In simple cooperation, and even in that based on the division of labor, the elimination of isolated work by the collective worker still seems more or less accidental. Machinism [...] functions only through socialized or shared labor. The cooperative nature of work becomes a technical necessity dictated by the very nature of its means."

MODERN MACHINISM REQUIRES THE DEVELOPMENT OF THE COOPERATIVE NATURE OF WORK. What was only possible accidentally becomes a necessity. But at the same time, it must be emphasized, what alone gives machinismo its value is the transformation of the social relations of production (the division of labor). Machinism both makes it possible to place thousands and tens of thousands of workers under a single command, and demands it; the machine is not there to alleviate human suffering, but to increase profit. Machinism has no productivity of its own, since it "functions only

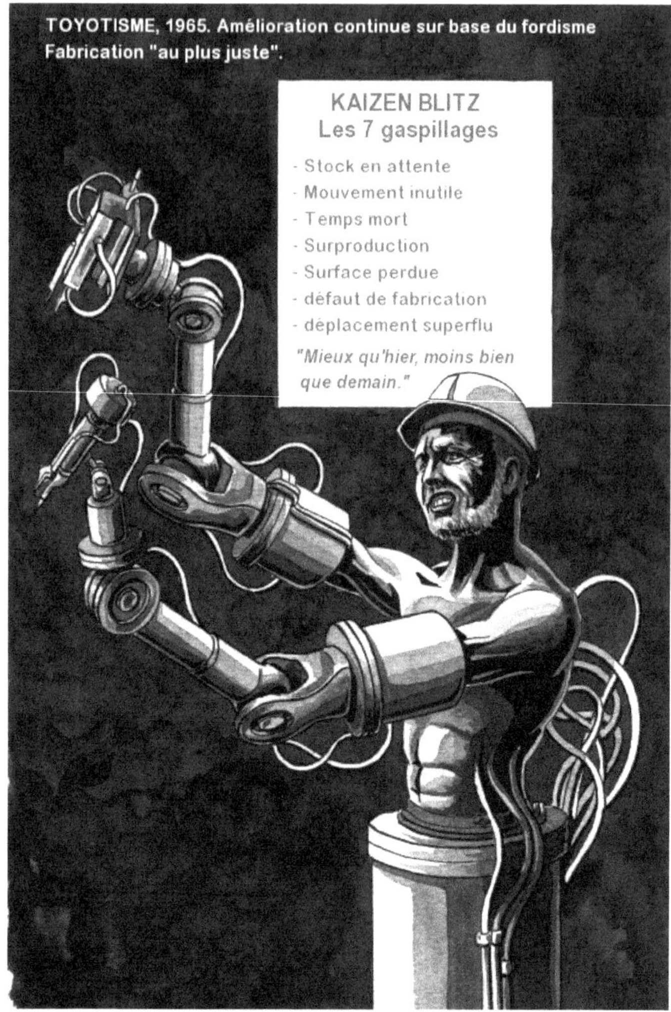

TOYOTISME, 1965. Amélioration continue sur base du fordisme
Fabrication "au plus juste".

KAIZEN BLITZ
Les 7 gaspillages

- Stock en attente
- Mouvement inutile
- Temps mort
- Surproduction
- Surface perdue
- défaut de fabrication
- déplacement superflu

"Mieux qu'hier, moins bien
que demain."

by means of socialized labor". And yet, in the capitalist production process, the productivity of labor is attributed to the machine.

TO SUM UP, CAPITALISM IS THE WORLD TURNED UPSIDE DOWN. Instead of the economy serving to produce the means of life, the means of life become the means for economic development and the accumulation of money. Instead of the worker using the means of labor, it's as if the worker becomes the means of the means of labor. In this way, the worker's personal power is converted into the objective power of capital, which can still be called "alienation".

6

Class Struggle and Domination

To understand the capitalist relationship, that relationship of subordination of labor to capital, is not only to discover the mystery of the transformation of money into capital (or of the self-engendering of money). It also means beginning to understand what "class struggle" is all about. In the capitalist mode of production, classes are not fixed social entities. Discussions about the existence or disappearance of the working class, or the position of employees, managers and technicians in the social hierarchy, are likely to be idle. Here again, caricatured representations of Marxism must be discarded. The evolution of capitalism, largely anticipated by Marx, shows this. The essential thing is the capitalist relationship itself: the exchange of money for the commodity "labor power" and the productive consumption of this commodity create the relationship of domination and the "class relationship", if we want to keep the terminology enshrined in the Marxist tradition. This class relation becomes manifest when workers enter into struggle against the logic of capital. Struggles over working hours are a case in point. "The capitalist upholds his right as a buyer when he seeks to extend the working day as long as possible and make two days out of one. On the other hand, the special nature of the commodity sold demands that its consumption by the buyer is not unlimited, and the worker supports his right as seller when he wants to restrict the working day to a normally determined duration. There is thus an antinomy here, right versus right, both bearing the stamp of the law that regulates the exchange of goods. Between two equal rights, who decides? Force." Social classes exist and are determined by this struggle, the consequence of the wage relationship. We could say that **it's not classes that enter into struggle, but the struggle that makes classes. And individuals arrange themselves around this "class struggle" operator**.

It's not enough to be very rich to be a capitalist. A soccer or singing star can earn a lot of money, but that doesn't make him or her a capitalist. Conversely, as we have already noted, gigantic amounts of capital do not belong to private capitalists, but come from the centralization of

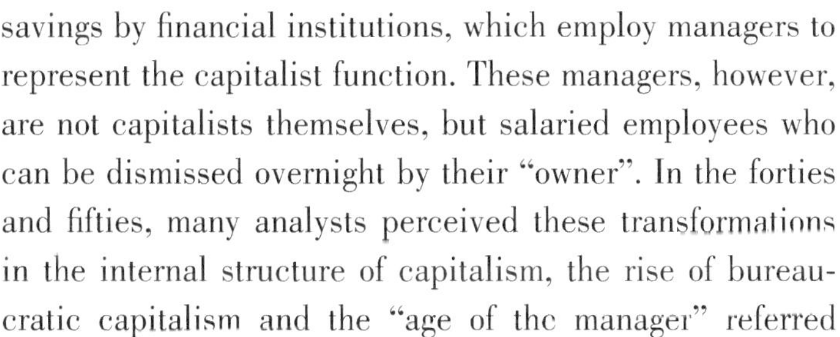

savings by financial institutions, which employ managers to represent the capitalist function. These managers, however, are not capitalists themselves, but salaried employees who can be dismissed overnight by their "owner". In the forties and fifties, many analysts perceived these transformations in the internal structure of capitalism, the rise of bureaucratic capitalism and the "age of the manager" referred to by James Burnham. But this transformation, far from leading from capitalism to a "post-capitalism", ultimately completed the capitalist relationship, again following paths indicated by Marx.

The "old-style" capitalist had (and still has in small businesses) a dual nature. On the one hand, as the owner of capital, he is the one who pockets the profit and derives his social power from it. But on the other, he directs the production process, fulfilling a necessary function—a function found in all modes of production. With the development of credit and joint-stock companies—forms which in their own way represent a certain "socialization" of capital—the purely capitalist function and the direction of the production process are separated. The manager and the capitalist are now two distinct characters. This can be seen as a virtual overcoming of capitalism: since the owner of capital is now outside the production process, it's not complicated to dispense with him and entrust the direction of the economy to the "associated producers", from the manager down to the laborer. But this virtuality, on which Marx effectively closes Book I of *Capital,* is not the only one. The separation of capital and production frees capital to move unhindered from one sector of production to another, from one enterprise to another. The capitalist is no longer tied to "his" tool of labor; he is no longer even tied to production itself. Whatever the method used, what matters to the capitalist is the "return on investment" that comes from the competitive advantages given by innovation or pure speculation, the conquest of new markets or vile trafficking.

At the same time, the barriers to capital's domination disappear with this "absolute capitalism". Capitalism, which had developed within a national framework, seems to have completely emancipated itself from this framework, moving very rapidly to low-wage, high-profit zones. At the same time, workers' resistance is weakening: they remain rooted in their national framework, they know no language other than their own, and their only asset is the social laws that protect them.

WEALTH IN OUR SOCIETIES MAY APPEAR TO BE AN IMMENSE ACCUMULATION OF COMMODITIES, BUT WE NEED TO SEPARATE WEALTH FROM COMMODITIES. **The earth, air, water, landscapes and natural resources, including those of human nature, are non-commodity wealth, wealth because they are goods that are useful to life or make it more pleasant, but wealth that has not yet entered the round of exchange.** Within the family circle, relationships are still governed by a division of tasks based on tradition or consciously decided (one takes out the trash, the other does the dishes, the third irons the shirts...). But a

QUI PREND SOIN DE VOUS?
Votre foyer mérite nos experts !!!
Forfait prestation
longue durée !!!

considerable part of family production has already fallen into the orbit of commodity production: meal preparation, which is giving way to industrial food. The commodification of the living is well underway, not to mention the market in human procreation that is opening up with the gradual legalization of surrogate motherhood. The development of "absolute capitalism" tends to transform all wealth into a commodity, and to make its production or conservation a field for the valorization of capital.

THIS INFINITE EXTENSION OF THE FIELD OF CAPITALIST DOMINATION IS THE LOGICAL PRODUCT OF THE LAWS OF CAPITAL ACCUMULATION. To want capitalism without accepting its consequences, as advocated by all the defenders of a supposedly moralized or regulated capitalism, is at best a perfectly utopian vision, at worst a discourse to lull to sleep those who might be tempted to revolt against this system.

La mondialisation heureuse
WTO OMC
INTERNATIONAL MONETARY FUND
Coca-Cola

7

Internal Contradictions of the Capitalist Mode of Production

For Marx, it's not just a question of describing how the capitalist mode of production works, but also of producing a critique that paves the way for its overthrow. Early socialist and anarchist utopias described an ideal society as opposed to capitalist society, depicted as hell. Marx took a radically different approach. He wants to show that capitalism is doomed not because it is evil or immoral, but because of its own internal development. **Capital is not a thing, but a social relation,** and this social relation is, in its essence, contradictory. We'll explain why in a moment, but for Marx, the development of this contradiction would lead to the abolition of the capitalist relation, with the same necessity that presides over the metamorphoses of nature.

FORDLANDIA, au cœur de l'Amazonie. Projet de ville industrielle entrepris par Henry Ford en 1927, abandonné en 1945.

THIS IS WHERE THINGS GET REALLY COMPLICATED, AND WHERE THE MISUNDERSTANDINGS OF MARX'S THINKING BEGIN. If the capitalist mode of production is doomed to disappear and give way to communism as fatally as chrysalises become butterflies, there's nothing left to do but wait for History (capitalized, please!) to do its work. But Marx says it over and over again:

History doesn't do anything, because History is merely the succession of generations. It's people who make their own history, even if it's in circumstances they haven't chosen, which they inherit from previous generations. Between the determinism and fatalism implied by some of Marx's formulations, and the idea of the free action of individuals, the true subjects of history, it's hard to find one's bearings. Which interpretation should we choose?

To this should be added what historical experience teaches us: not only has the capitalist mode of production not collapsed, a victim of its own contradictions, but it also seems to have succeeded in putting down all its challengers. Anarchist utopias were revealed for what they were: utopias, places of nowhere. Traditional socialism passed from Marxism to the "social market economy" and "global governance", losing the last traces of socialism. Communism in the 20th century collapsed in two years, almost without serious convulsions: it had been dead for a long time, and the corpse turned to dust with the first flick of a switch from East Berlin. In the end, Marx wouldn't even have been a match for Nostradamus.

But in reality, it's something else. **The "commodity form" itself contains the possibility of an interruption in circulation, and therefore of a crisis:** it is always possible that the producer of commodities will find no buyer on the market, and that the social value of his work will collapse or even be reduced to nothing. Conversely, when buyers outnumber sellers, the possibility exists of a speculative bubble forming. This formal possibility, which is as old as the market economy—see the famous tulip crisis of 1636—becomes a real possibility in the capitalist mode of production.

The fundamental law of capital is the law of accumulation. Capital is invested in order to increase, and so it must constantly find new means of existence: it must find fields of accumulation, i.e. sectors where production can meet growing demand, otherwise each individual capital will seek to supplant its neighbor to take its "market share". All this is easy to observe experimentally. As capital moves forward, it is confronted with the need to capture more and more surplus value, and this can be done in two ways. Firstly, by increasing the number of workers employed at a sufficiently high rate of exploitation and, secondly, by increasing the rate of exploitation, which can be done either by lengthening the working day (but this encounters unsurpassable physical limits), or by increasing the proportion of free labor in a working day—i.e., by reducing the proportion of wages, by lowering wages below the socially recognized level (a solution difficult to put into practice in the long term) or by reducing the value of the commodities needed to reproduce labor power, as we saw above.

THESE METHODS OF GUARANTEEING CAPITAL ACCUMULATION HAVE SEVERAL CONSEQUENCES.

The first, the best-known and least questionable, is the concentration and centralization of capital. Concentration: some take over from others, or simply eliminate them. Centralization: all available capital, i.e. all sums of money likely to function as capital, are "socialized" (as in the case of joint-stock companies) or centralized in the hands of financial institutions, banks, investment funds, pension funds, insurance companies, etc. For capitalist ideology, production must be a matter of free enterprise and individual responsibility, and its founding myth is that of the *"self-made man"*, a well-known "robinsonnade". But, **empirically speaking, capital can only survive by continually extending the boundaries of capitalist private property**.

The tendency to overproduction is the second fundamental expression of the contradictions of the capitalist mode of production. The capitalist is a fanatic of production for production's sake: the more goods that come out of his factories, the more he can make his capital bear fruit. The

multiplication of supply is the key to this mode of production. It's not for nothing that supply-side policies once again came to the fore in the last two decades of the previous century, after a long Keynesian interlude based on demand-side policies. But of course, this supply has to find buyers.

And buyers must have, firstly, the means to buy, and secondly, the need or desire to buy.

For the first condition, it's easy to see that the great mass of purchasers of consumer goods are wage earners... about whom the individual capitalist is not at all keen that they should be paid more to buy the goods produced by other capitalists. Every capitalist would be quite in favor of increasing the "purchasing power" of other capitalists' wage earners, as long as it didn't give his own wage earners the wrong idea.

As for the second condition, we can also see its very empirical manifestations. When a family has two cars and three televisions, it will be hard to convince them to increase their equipment. Hence the need to increase the speed with which goods are renewed (for consumption as well as production). **This means making the latest equipment obsolete as quickly as possible, limiting its lifespan and encouraging people to consume more and more. And when economic means aren't enough, we turn to the State, which itself organizes the destruction of goods in need of renewal** (e.g.: the "scrappage bonus" for cars, or the imposition of new standards).

Third major trend: the race for labor productivity. If a capitalist can produce in one hour what is usually done in two hours, given that the value of goods is measured in terms of the time socially required to produce them, this capitalist will be able to pocket more than the average profit. But this has two drawbacks: firstly, increasing productivity generally requires new technical means, i.e. an increase in constant capital; secondly, after a certain time, the other capitalists competing with our innovator either disappear, or are absorbed by the stronger group. In other words, on the one hand, the race for productivity, which is fundamentally *"labor-saving"*, ends up undermining the basis for the production of surplus-value, since surplus-value is and can only be born of living labor. On the other hand, competition naturally gives way to monopolies (or, at least, oligopolies), and the free initiative of individuals builds the huge bureaucracies of multinational firms.

All these contradictory tendencies of the capitalist mode of production explain why it is both revolutionary and deadly. Revolutionary, because it can only survive by constantly revolutionizing modes of production, by continually overturning habits, by ruthlessly destroying all that was taken for intangible. As early as the 1848 *Manifesto*, Marx celebrated the revolutionary character of the capitalist mode of production. But it is also a deadly mode of production. By substituting dead labor for living labor, capital accumulation leads to crisis, or rather to repeated crises—the famous "cyclical crises" that are the *"memento mori"* ("remember that you must die") of capitalism. The crisis brutally devalues all existing capital, unsaleable goods are sent to the dump, and labor power is left fallow. Wars provide a not inconsiderable field for capital accumulation—the arms industry plays a key role in the economies of all the major capitalist countries—and at the same time destroy commodities, allowing them to be renewed and the productive apparatus to be rebuilt on new foundations. As can be seen, the entire history of the 20th century supports the analysis and predictions made by Marx in the second half of the 19th century.

8

False Exit Routes

If capitalism hasn't collapsed, say its defenders, it's because it's highly efficient and flexible, and has shown a capacity for adaptation that no other mode of production in the past has been able to demonstrate. In short, far from being doomed, as Marx thought, this mode of production is, on the contrary, the one that marks the "end of history": nothing could be better, and even the French Socialists made it their "historical horizon" at a congress in 1991.

However, the reality of the situation is a little less glamorous than what is said in the land of the thurifers of triumphant capitalism. The last century saw the bloody crises of the capitalist mode of production, and the methods used to organize its rescue have little in common with the apologetic fables of the purported "economic liberalism".

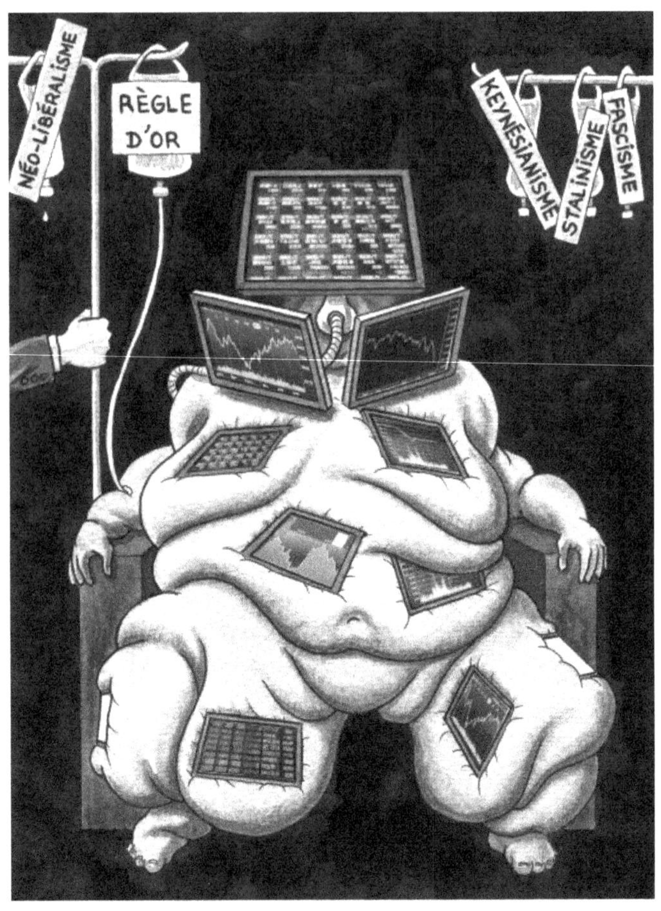

NÉO-LIBÉRALISME
RÈGLE D'OR
KEYNÉSIANISME
STALINISME
FASCISME

The First World War can be seen as the first violent explosion of the capitalist mode of production. Capitalist development based on the imperialist expansion of the great European powers led to a deadly clash between English, Russian and French imperialism on the one hand, and German and Austrian imperialism on the other. Unprecedented destruction and a war that became a world war for the first time. A war in which all the modern industrial means of destruction were invented, and in which the whole process of civilization carried forward by the Europeans, with more or less legitimate claims, collapsed under the rain of shells, asphyxiating gas and attacks on civilian populations. The dream of the Enlightenment died in the trenches of Verdun.

The war also laid the foundations for what came to be known ambiguously as state capitalism: in all the major capitalist countries, industry and the state apparatus were closely intertwined. Cannon merchants profited from the war, but the state apparatus began to take over the running of the economic machine. This is why Lenin sees nationalization and planning under Soviet state control as a simple extension of what the evolution of the capitalist mode of production had already outlined.

For many observers, the crisis of 1929 seemed to be the "final crisis" that Marx (wrongly) predicted. **The**

ordinary cyclical crises that punctuated the course of business were giving way to a major crisis of the system itself. The classic model of the liberal state and the market economy seemed to be dying. Many intellectuals, convinced by the facts, rallied to Marxism—it was at this time that the Soviet secret services recruited quite extensively from Britain's most prestigious universities, providing some of the most high-profile espionage cases after the Second World War and the material for John Le Carré's first novels. At the other end of the spectrum, those who rejected "communism"—or at least what presented itself under that label—advocated another form of revolution, exemplified by Italian Fascism and German Nazism.

Fascism and Nazism, each in its own way, proposed to safeguard capitalist property by continuing to the end the process of unification outlined during the war. This meant liquidating not only workers' organizations and anything that might appear "communist", but also basic democratic freedoms. Nazism added its own special touch with racial theories and the destruction of European Jewry. The United States under Roosevelt and France under the Front Populaire offered a third solution to the crisis that began in 1929, by organizing and regulating capital, collaborating with the unions and giving a key role to Keynesian-inspired government economic policies.

In short, between communism (in fact, the Stalinist system), fascism and Keynesian interventionism, the classical capitalist mode of production gave way to the "bureaucratization of the world" (the expression is coined by the Italian revolutionary Bruno Rizzi) which, in various forms, condemned outright the idea that the economic dynamics of capital accumulation were sufficient to ensure peace and prosperity. These were attempts to rescue capitalism from itself—Soviet-style experiments can be included in this rescue effort, for in Russia as in China, so-called communism was essentially a brutal means of moving from a backward society to a new kind of capitalism. Indirectly and rather unexpectedly, it was still Marx's prognosis that had come true, and by no means proof of capitalism's resilience.

But once again, **war appeared as the fatal outcome of the explosive contradictions accumulated by the contradictory development of global capitalism**. A war that ravaged Europe and part of Asia, and was prolonged by the Cold War and the multiple, often devastating conflicts it served as a backdrop to. The unglamorous demise of the "real socialist" regimes at the end of the 1980s brought this episode to a close, ushering in a period of euphoria for the spokesmen of capital. Marx was dead and the end of history was capitalist. We were going to be able to

return to true capitalism, with free competition and the
disengagement of the state. But nothing came of it. Crises
from the Internet "bubble" of 2002 to the *subprime* crisis
have shown that the capitalist mode of production remains

caught up in the contradictions analyzed by Marx. *Marx is back*," ran the headline in many major newspapers in 2008, and *Capital* enjoyed a marked revival. The Archbishop of Canterbury, Rowan Williams, hardly suspected of Marxist sympathies, believes that "Marx has long observed the way in which savage capitalism has become a kind of myth, ascribing reality and power to act to things that had no life in themselves; he's right about that". According to *Time* magazine of January 22, 2009, the spectre of Karl Marx haunts the world "from Washington to Vladivostok".

9

Why the Capitalist Mode
of Production is Doomed

OSTRICH-POLITICIANS AND LIARS FOR HIRE ASIDE, EVERYONE KNOWS THAT THE EMERGENCY RESCUE MEASURES TAKEN TO DEAL WITH THE CONSEQUENCES OF THE *SUBPRIME* CRISIS HAVE SOLVED NOTHING. And the crisis is far from being just a financial crisis that can be curbed by prudent measures and fair regulation of capitalism. The crisis concerns the capitalist system itself, i.e. the possibility of unlimited capital accumulation. If the global economy is in danger of collapsing at any moment under the weight of derivatives and speculative capital of all kinds, it's not the fault of bad capitalists, ugly speculators or horrible *traders* (such as Société Générale *trader* Jérôme Kerviel). On the contrary, all these forms of speculation are developing because capital invested in direct productive activities is finding it increasingly difficult to be valorized at a sufficient rate of profit. Derivatives" offer investors the chance to pocket profits immediately, in the hope that they will actually be made in the future. What is the lesson here? Quite simply that speculative madness is a logical consequence of the imperative of unlimited capital accumulation, and by no means a perversion or disease of a fundamentally healthy system. Speculation destroying the productive system would be enough to sign the death warrant of the capitalist system.

But there's much more and much worse. **The unlimited accumulation of capital is obviously impossible.** Since the 15th century, the capitalist system has extended its hold over every continent and every sector of social life. Recent decades have seen a massive influx of peripheral countries into the very heart of the system. So much so, in fact, that they are becoming serious competitors for the declining old imperialist powers. After Asia, Africa has yet to be fully integrated, but Antarctica is unlikely to be a prolific field for capital accumulation! Unlimited accumulation, a condition of capitalism's survival, is incompatible with the finiteness of the planet, its resources and the possibilities humans have to inhabit it.

Homo Capitalis Panurgus
XVIIIème siècle - 20??

10. Communism

But this recognition of the impossibility of unlimited accumulation could lead only to a moral condemnation of capitalism, and possibly to authoritarian solutions, such as those advocated by certain ecologists, who propose treating people like children, holding them in fear and forcing them to restrain their insatiable appetites. Nothing of the sort is to be found in Marx, for whom condemnation of the capitalist mode of production must not lead to regression, but to an overcoming of it, which is *communism*.

The name *communism* is very old, predating Marx, and the idea is even older: in Plato's *Republic*, there's a kind of paradoxical communism, a communism aimed at the elite, i.e. the guardians of the city. The first Christian communities were typically communist: their members had to throw away all their possessions and participate fully in the common life.

With the birth of capitalism came new communist utopias, dreams of "sharers", of fraternal communities free of inequality and domination. But Marx began by rejecting this communism of the past. "We must let the dead bury their dead", says the Gospel. Marx's communism is not an ingenious plan for society to be implemented under the direction of "social engineers". It is the "real movement" unfolding before our very eyes. The fact that so-called "communist" parties are moribund or have simply disappeared does not alter this reality: communism emerges, as it were, spontaneously from the very movement of capitalist development.

In the first place, the capitalist mode of production has socialized production on a gigantic scale. Technical inventions are obviously of the utmost importance, but what constitutes the essential productive force that capitalism has developed is the cooperation of an ever-increasing number of producers on what is now a global scale. When it comes to exoteric economics, that of the economists and commentators in the financial press, the economy appears only as a battleground occupied by fierce adversaries who are always ready for a fight: the economy would be the continuation of war by other means, but competition on a global scale between all capitalist firms also covers ever-closer cooperation, to the point where it's

impossible to say that a French car came off a production line located in France, so many components come from China, Japan, Portugal, Germany or the UK. There is therefore a potentially violent conflict between this increasing socialization of the productive process and the private nature of capitalist appropriation.

Let's put the problem another way. As we have said, the extension of production, at a certain stage, becomes possible only through the massive development of credit and "fictitious capital", and through the centralization of capital by means of joint-stock companies. Both of these signal the virtual disappearance of the capitalist mode of production. They result in the radical separation of capital ownership from the functions performed by the capitalist. It is the manager, salaried by the owners of capital, who replaces the capitalist in all aspects of supervisory and managerial work. This work has two aspects. On the one hand, it is productive work, necessary in any production system that requires the coordination of the work of a large number of individuals. On the other hand, it is closely linked to any mode of production based on antagonism between social classes, insofar as it is necessary to guarantee the domination of the dominant.

Thus, "capitalist production has reached a point where managerial labor, completely separated from the ownership of capital, is running the streets, so that the capitalist no longer needs to fulfill this function himself". In other words, it is the very development of capitalist production that has rendered the capita-

list superfluous, turning him into a parasite on production. Experiments with workers' cooperatives provide positive proof of this reality. Hence the conclusion: "On the one hand, the sole owner of capital, the financial capitalist, finds himself face to face with the active capitalist, and, thanks to the extension of credit, monetary capital takes on a social character: it is concentrated in banks and lent out by them and no longer directly by its owners; on the other hand, the sole manager, not being the owner of capital in any capacity —neither as borrower nor otherwise—effectively performs all the functions that fall to the active capitalist as such. It is then that, as a superfluous character, the capitalist disappears from the production process, and only the civil servant remains."

THE HISTORICALLY PROGRESSIVE FUNCTION OF THE CAPITALIST MODE OF PRODUCTION IS THUS COMING TO AN END. Everything is ready for the final scene. Even if most of the players, obsessed by what's happening on the surface, don't realize it.

Let's look at the problem from yet another angle. The capitalist mode of production is based on the extortion of surplus value from living labor. But on the other hand, as it develops, it also develops mechanization, reducing ever further the share of living labor in production. Although it encounters physical and technological limits, some of which may be insurmountable, the automation of the production process continues to progress. We need to integrate more and more workers into the production process—capital is the Moloch that feeds on living labor—and, at the same time, we need to save more and more human labor. Machinism reduces the amount of work required, while at the same time demanding more and more surplus labor.

In this way, growing social wealth, materialized in increasingly powerful machines, presents itself to living labor as a foreign, hostile power. **Scientific discoveries and new technical processes, far from alleviating human suffering as the thinkers of the seventeenth and eighteenth centuries believed, more often than not appear as real calamities to be suffered by workers**: some are thrown out into the street—and there's a lot to be said for the structural unemployment of contemporary capitalism—while others see their pace increased, the qualification of work reduced and the means of surveillance, i.e. the worker's submission to capital, considerably increased.

But this opposition between the objective "body" formed by production and immediate labor, i.e. the individual power of the worker, is bound to be overcome. It is a phase of human history, not an eternal necessity. What characterizes this historical and therefore transitional phase of capitalism is the growing contradiction between real wealth and value. As the automation of industrial processes and the division of labor develop, "real wealth depends less on labor time and the quantum of labor employed than on the power of the agents set in motion during labor time, which in turn bears no relation to the labor time immediately expended in producing them, but depends rather on the general level of science and the progress of technology, in other words, on the application of this science to production".

If the value of a commodity is coagulated labor time, at the same time social wealth manifests itself in the "extraordinary disproportion between labor time used and its product". The contradiction here is obvious: the lowering of production costs in a whole range of sectors has regularly led to a collapse in prices (particularly in the case of *"high-tech"* products), a collapse that drives manufacturers to seek out new, more efficient processes, and thus to continue a spiral that is constantly reducing the long-term profitability of these industries. But this fall in prices (and value) is accompanied by an increase in social wealth, conceived in terms of use values, i.e. goods that people can use easily.

The source of this wealth is the "social individual", and so the "theft of other people's working time, on which present wealth rests, seems a miserable basis compared to the newly developed wealth created by large-scale industry itself". In other words, large-scale industry, the product of cooperation and the socialization of production, is at odds with capitalist private property, which was the basis of its development.

This development of the power of social labor both makes possible and demands a fundamental transformation of social relations. As soon as production based on exchange value collapses—and this is the root cause of today's endemic "crisis"—"mass surplus-labor ceases to be the condition for the development of general wealth", and the possibility of radical emancipation opens up for individuals: "It is the free development of individualities, where society's necessary working time is not reduced in order to pose overwork, but where society's necessary work is reduced to a minimum, to which artistic, scientific, etc., training corresponds., of individuals thanks to the time freed up and the means created by all of them".

In this way, the capitalist mode of production has created the conditions for radical individual emancipation, a real possibility that can only be realized by harmonizing social relations and the development of the social individual. This possibility is called *communism*, but obviously in a very different sense from traditional communism: far from being the absorption of the individual into the collectivity, this communism is an "individualist" communism, in the sense that it aims for the fulfillment of the individual, who is his own end; far from the frugal ideals of earlier communisms, it assumes, on the contrary, the maximum development of social wealth.

Finally, if the development of capitalist production relations leads to the creation of a collective worker and a collective intelligence, this in turn makes possible the expropriation of capitalists and the transition to communism. The accumulation of capital has turned "the dwarf property of the many into the colossal property of the few", through an "appalling expropriation of the working people". This concentration enables the application of science and techno-logy to large-scale production, and favors "the interweaving of peoples in the network of the universal market". But this process is contradictory: **"The monopoly of capital becomes a hindrance to the mode of production that has grown and prospered with it and under its auspices. The socialization of labor and the centra-lization of its material resources have reached a point where they can no longer fit into their capitalist envelope. That envelope is shattering. The time for capitalist ownership has come. The expropriators are in turn expropriated.**

Why is this possible? Because the capitalist has lost his necessary function in the organization of production to "civil servants", managers and executives. The capitalist thus becomes superfluous and can be replaced by the "association of producers", from the director to the mainte-nance worker, an association of which workers' cooperatives form the outline, even if, in the environment of an economy dominated by the capitalist mode of production, they cannot remain islands of communism for long.

11

How it Works

From the analysis of social relations, we have arrived at a historical perspective. But this is not a philosophy of history: Marx does not promise a radiant future that would flow almost naturally from the movement of concepts. Capital, labor, value, etc., all the terms we've just conceived and developed, are not things at all, but the theoretical expression of social relationships, i.e. relationships between living individuals. Economic categories do nothing, history does nothing. Only individuals act, and they don't act like puppets manipulated by structures beyond their control; they act on the basis of their own determinations, their own feelings, their own subjective vision of reality. If you want to understand something of what Marx was trying to think, you always have to go back there. It's usually said—and this is how Marxism is presented, and how Marxists very often present themselves—that Marx is a materialist, because for him the economy would determine social life and the life of the mind. But this is not the case. Economics, thought through the categories of economics, is nothing especially material. Nothing is less material than money. The "material basis", if we can call it that, is the practical activity of individuals acting in relation to other individuals, and acting first and foremost to continue to exist as living beings, which presupposes food, clothing and a few other things besides...

IF WE NOW RETURN TO THE HISTORY OF CAPITALISM, WE UNDERSTAND THAT IT CANNOT DISAPPEAR OF ITS OWN ACCORD, a victim of its own internal contradictions. The very evolution of the capitalist mode of production opens up possibilities, but in no way guarantees a necessary denouement of this history. Possibilities can only be realized if the great mass of individuals make them their objective, the meaning of their actions. People make their own history, even if it's under conditions they haven't chosen. But they don't make this history from pre-established plans, or from a "theoretical consciousness" that would make them the conscious agents of "historical necessity". We can dismiss providence without remorse! We can also give up on the "great evening" once and for all. No supreme savior (nor God, nor Caesar, nor tribune, as the song goes), none of those multiple leaders, great or small, who

«Les philosophes n'ont fait qu'interpréter diversement le monde,
il s'agit maintenant de le transformer.» (Karl Marx)

claim to be the spokesmen of the revolutionary movement, is to be expected. No eschatology, no messianism. If communism is in the real movement, it is in those who, through collective action, fight concretely to abolish the competition between workers to sell their labor power (what Marx properly calls wage-labor). The real movement is to be found in those partial associations that enable "those below to resist", in those who want to escape the shackles of capitalist enterprise by exploring alternative paths, and in all concrete initiatives to organize social transformation here and now, in modes of production, in distribution, in cultural action.

The Greeks called it *praxis*, the practical activity by which men transform themselves, a term that Marx adopts as his own. Marx's thought is indeed a "philosophy of praxis", and this is the key to his singular communism.

Table of Contents

www.ingramcontent.com/pod-product-compliance
Lightning Source LLC
LaVergne TN
LVHW051200060726
842526LV00014B/3299